# Essential Physical Science

# MAGNETISM

**Louise and Richard Spilsbury**

Chicago, Illinois

© 2014 Heinemann Library
an imprint of Capstone Global Library, LLC
Chicago, Illinois

To contact Capstone Global Library, please call 800-747-4992, or visit our web site, www.capstonepub.com

Edited by Andrew Farrow and Abby Colich
Designed by Cynthia Akiyoshi
Original illustrations © Capstone Global Library Ltd 2014
Illustrated by HL Studios
Picture research by Tracy Cummins
Originated by Capstone Global Library Ltd
Printed in China by China Translation and Printing Services

17 16 15 14 13
10 9 8 7 6 5 4 3 2

**Library of Congress Cataloging-in-Publication Data**

Spilsbury, Richard, 1963-
  Magnetism / Richard and Louise Spilsbury.
    p. cm.
  Summary: "Everyone is familiar with magnets, but how much do we know about how they actually work? This book explores the basics of magnets, looking at topics such as poles, electromagnets, and how we use the Earth's magnetic field to find our way."—Provided by publisher.
  Includes bibliographical references and index.
  ISBN 978-1-4329-8148-8 (hb)—ISBN 978-1-4329-8157-0 (pb)  1. Magnetism—Juvenile literature.  I. Spilsbury, Louise. II. Title.

QC753.7.S65 2014
538—dc23                    2013011759

## Acknowledgments

We would like to thank the following for permission to reproduce photographs: Alamy: p. 31 (© Caro); Capstone Library: pp. 7 (Karon Dubke), 10 (Karon Dubke), 11 (Karon Dubke), 14 (Karon Dubke), 16 (Karon Dubke), 24 (Karon Dubke), 25 (Karon Dubke), 40 (Karon Dubke), 41 (Karon Dubke); Corbis: p. 38 (© Imaginechina); Getty Images: pp. 17 (Martin Leigh), 27 (Science Images/UIG), 29 (Image Source), 30 (Ecc Images), 32 (Monty Rakusen), 33 (Arnt Haug); 37 (Ingram Publishing); Nasa: p. 43; newscom: pp. 19 (Splash News), 39 (suministrada/El Nuevo Dia de Puerto Rico); Photo Researchers: pp. 12 (Spencer Grant), 18 (Cordelia Molloy / Science Source), 22 (Scott Camazine), 26 (Doug Martin / Science Source); Shutterstock: pp. 6 (© Borislav Toskov), 9 (© Krom), 13 (© dondesigns), 21 (© corepics), 35 (© Zadorozhnyi Viktor); Superstock: pp. 4 (BE&W), 5 (imagebroker.net), 20 (Axiom Photographic Limited), 42 (imagebroker.net).

Cover image of a cluster of iron fillings being attracted by a horseshoe magnet reproduced with permission from Photo Researchers (Tek Image / Science Source).

Every effort has been made to contact copyright holders of material reproduced in this book. Any omissions will be rectified in subsequent printings if notice is given to the publisher.

## Disclaimer

# Contents

## Eureka moment!

Learn about important discoveries that have brought about further knowledge and understanding.

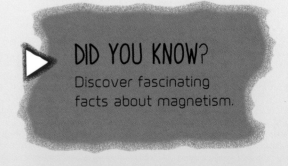

## DID YOU KNOW?

Discover fascinating facts about magnetism.

## WHAT'S NEXT?

Read about the latest research and advances in essential physical science.

Some words are shown in bold, **like this**. You can find out what they mean by looking in the glossary.

# What Is Magnetism?

Magnetism is a **force** we use every day without really knowing it is there. A force is something that can pull or push on an object. A **magnet** can pull on iron paper clips to lift them up and it can push on another magnet to make it jump or slide away from it. If you have ever played with magnets, you know that they stick to each other and to some types of metals.

## Using magnets

There are magnets inside the edges of refrigerator doors too, helping to keep them closed! Magnets help to make many things work. Magnets are often found in can openers, holding the lid to the opener, and many bags have magnetic clasps to hold them shut. There are magnets in doorbells, telephones, and televisions, and computers and CD players use magnets too. Magnetism is also used in electric **motors** that make machines like food mixers and electric toothbrushes work.

When you hold a magnet close to a refrigerator door, you can feel the force of magnetism pulling it toward the metal door.

## Eureka!

More than 2,000 years ago, the ancient Greeks found a **mineral** that attracted things made of iron. The word magnet probably comes from an area in Turkey called Magnesia, where the ancient Greeks found lots of these minerals in the ground.

ery powerful magnets can be used to lift and move very heavy objects. Here a large magnet is lifting heavy rolls of steel and loading them into a train.

# DID YOU KNOW?

Cows are not fussy eaters and sometimes swallow staples, nails, or other bits of metal when munching grass, so some farmers insert magnets into their stomachs. Metals stick to the magnets instead of moving about and puncturing the animals' internal organs.

# How Do Magnets Work?

Magnets work because they produce a magnetic force. This force is strongest near the ends of a magnet. These are called the **poles** of the magnet. One is a north pole, the other is a south pole. Different, or unlike, poles attract each other. So, if you put the south pole of one magnet near the north pole of another magnet, they pull together. Like poles **repel**. So if you bring two north or two south poles near each other, they try to push apart.

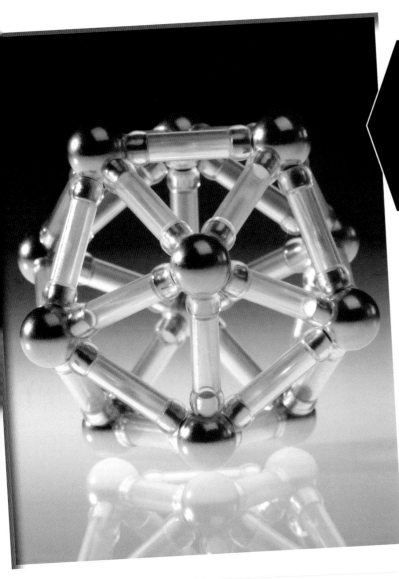

By putting north and south poles of magnetic rods and balls like this together, you can use their magnetic forces to pull together and hold large, intricate shapes.

## DID YOU KNOW?

If you don't know which end of a long bar magnet is its north pole, hang it from the middle on a string so it can spin. You will see that one end of the magnet always ends up pointing to the north. That's its north pole!

# Many magnets

Magnets can be different sizes and shapes. They can be round, rod-shaped, horseshoe-shaped, and in bars. Every magnet still has a north and south pole. When we use force to push or pull something we have to touch it, like when we kick a ball or pull the curtains. Magnetism does not need to touch things for its force to have an effect. Some magnets are so strong that their force can work through air, water, and even some solid things.

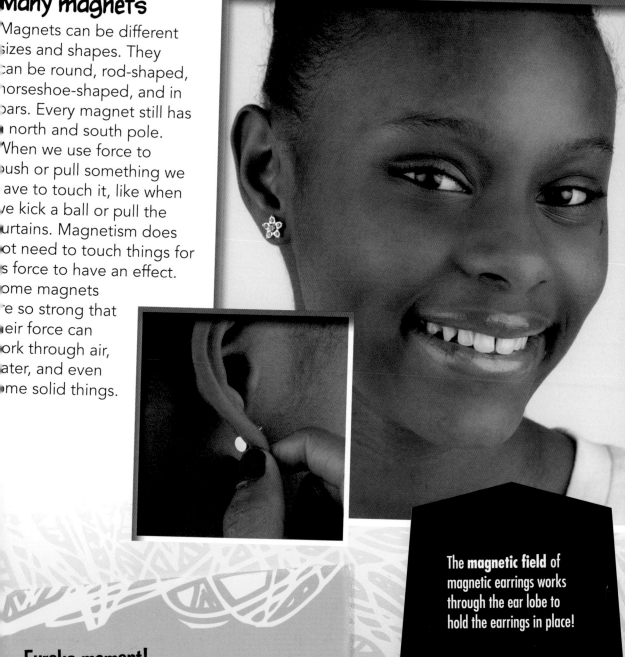

The **magnetic field** of magnetic earrings works through the ear lobe to hold the earrings in place!

## Eureka moment!

In 1777 French scientist Charles Coulomb (1736–1806) came up with a mathematical formula that showed that the strength of attraction between two magnets gets smaller and smaller the further away from each other they are.

# Inside a magnet

Why are some materials magnetic, while others are not? Some materials have areas of magnetic forces inside them, called magnetic **domains**. In a material that is magnetic, all of these tiny magnets are lined up and facing in the same direction. Together they create a strong pulling or pushing force. In a material that is not magnetic, these domains are all jumbled up and facing in many different directions. The mini magnets cancel each other out so there is no overall magnetic force.

## Eureka!

French scientist Pierre Weiss explained the domain theory in 1907, based on ideas by other scientists. He stated that all the magnetic forces in a material have to be lined up for it to be magnetic.

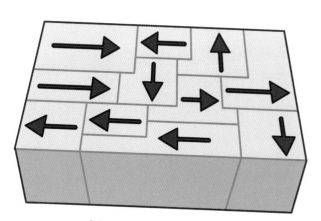

Unmagnetized

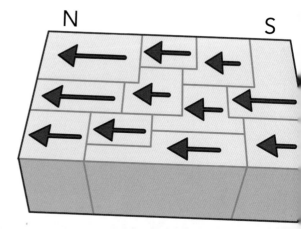

N

S

Magnetized

Domains are like tiny magnets of different sizes within an object. In this picture, magnetic domains are shown by arrows. Only when the domains are lined up and facing the same way is a metal magnetic.

## All lined up

It might help to think of magnets and nonmagnets as parking lots. In one, the cars are parked facing in different directions. When they turn on their headlights you see light coming from all over the place. This is like the domains in a nonmagnetic material. In the other parking lot, all the cars are facing in one direction and all their headlights are pointing in one direction too, making a powerful beam of light! This is how domains within a magnet are laid out.

You can imagine the domains in a magnet are lined up in an orderly way like these new cars in a lot!

# Try This!

The force of a magnet on something made of iron acts over a distance. But is the strength of that magnetism weaker when different or thicker materials are placed between the two objects?

## Prediction

Magnetism will be weaker when it passes through some materials than others.

## Equipment

- strong bar magnet
- 10 metal paper clips
- sheets of different materials such as paper, card, wood, plastic, and aluminum (these materials are not attracted to a magnet)
- pencil and paper

## Method

1 Prepare a record sheet like this one. In the first column under the first heading, write "Paper." Then in the second column, write what effect you think that material will have on the strength of the magnetism between the magnet and the paper clips. Then carry out the test, from step 2.

| Item | Prediction | Result |
|---|---|---|
| Paper | | |
| 5 sheets of paper | | |
| 10 sheets of paper | | |
| | | |
| | | |
| | | |

Test the effect of paper on the strength of the magnetism between the magnet and the paper clips by resting the paper clips on top of the paper and moving the magnet around underneath them. Can you make the magnet move the paper clips? Record what happened in the third column of the record sheet.

**3** Now test more sheets of paper, say 2 or 5, and list this in the first column of your record chart. Then test this amount in exactly the same way. First make a prediction, then do the test, and then record the results.

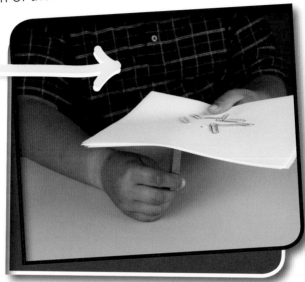

**4** Do the same tests for cardboard and add these to your record chart too.

**5** Now test the remaining materials and add these to your record chart too.

## Results

The force of magnetism passes more easily through some materials than others; for example it passes more easily through paper than wood. Also, the attraction between a magnet and something attracted to it is weaker across larger distances, so it passes more easily through a thin sheet of cardboard than several sheets of the same cardboard.

# What Are Magnetic Materials?

Magnetic materials are those that are attracted to magnets. Magnets attract some metals, but not all. The most common magnetic material is iron, but the metals nickel, cobalt, and most types of steel are attracted to magnets too. Many metals are not attracted to magnets, including copper, aluminum, gold, silver, tin, brass, and lead. Many other common materials are nonmagnetic too, such as paper, wood, plastic, and textiles.

## DID YOU KNOW?

Many of the breakfast cereals we eat have iron added to them. Our bodies need small amounts of iron to make healthy blood. Crush an iron-fortified breakfast cereal into a powder and use a strong magnet to check if it is high in iron!

Because magnets only attract certain magnetic materials, they can be used to separate iron and steel (magnetic materials) from aluminum waste at recycling plants.

# Making magnetic materials

Magnets are very useful, so people make new magnetic materials. Ferrite is a ceramic material made from magnetic powders such as iron oxide. Ferrites are used in radio antennas, and one type, called magnadur, is used to make the bar magnets often used in schools. Alnico is a magnetic material made from a mixture of aluminum, nickel, iron, and cobalt. It makes strong, long-lasting magnets.

## Eureka!

Alnico magnets were invented by Tokushichi Mishima of Japan in 1932. They are still used in many everyday objects, including magnetic compasses, telephone receivers, loudspeakers, and instruments that measure electric current.

Alnico magnets are used in electric guitar pickups. Pickups attach to guitars and capture vibrations from guitar strings and make the sounds louder (see page 34 for more on this).

# Making things magnetic

We can make materials that are attracted to magnets into magnets themselves. You can turn an iron nail into a magnet by rubbing a strong magnet several times over its surface. If you rub the magnet over the nail several times, the nail becomes a stronger magnet. This happens because as you rub the magnet over the nail, some of its magnetic domains line up (see pages 8–9) and the metal becomes a little bit magnetic. When you rub the magnet over the nail a lot, more of its magnetic domains line up and it becomes a stronger magnet!

## WHAT'S NEXT?

Some scientists are working on making liquids that can harden or change shape when they feel a magnetic field. They hope to use them to help make robots move their joints and limbs in a lifelike way in the future.

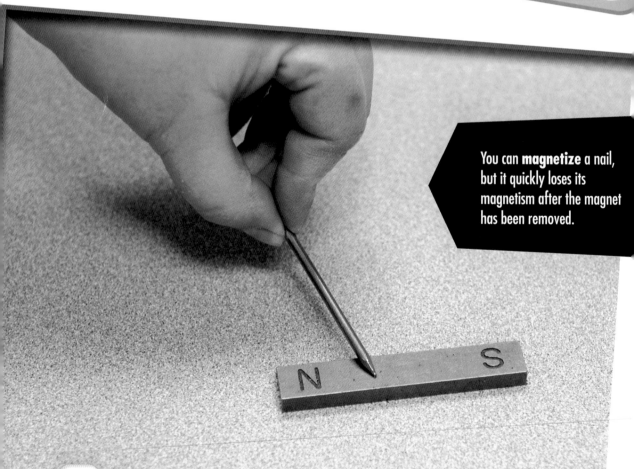

You can **magnetize** a nail, but it quickly loses its magnetism after the magnet has been removed.

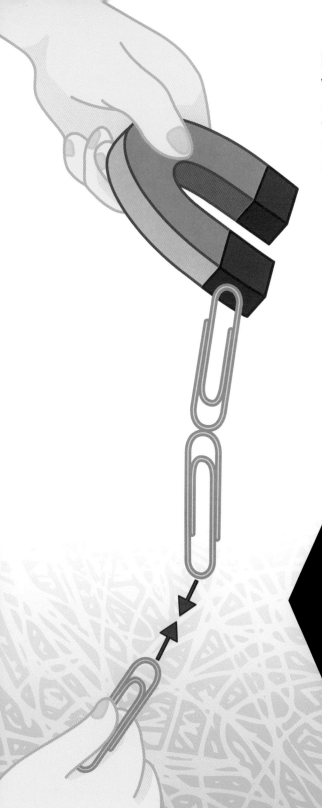

# Magnetic forces

When we know how to make materials magnetic, this helps us to understand how a magnet can pick up an unmagnetized object, such as a paper clip. Paper clips are usually made of iron, and when a magnet is close to a paper clip, the magnet pulls and lines up some of the domains in the paper clip. This makes the paper clip into a **temporary magnet** and the north pole of the paper clip becomes attracted toward the south pole of the magnet. When we take the magnet away, the domains of the paper clip return to being jumbled up and it loses its magnetic power.

You can make a paper clip chain by adding paper clips in a line from one hanging from a strong magnet. The clips become temporary magnets and attract others to them. How long does the chain stay together after you take away the magnet?

# Losing magnetism

You can **demagnetize** magnets, or make them lose their magnetism, too. This happens when the magnetic domains in a magnet move so that they are no longer lined up. Dropping a magnet or hitting it very hard can make it lose its magnetism. So can heating a magnet up. An iron magnet stops being a magnet if you heat it above 1300°F (770°C). You can also disrupt the domains of a magnet by moving another, stronger magnet repeatedly and in several directions across it.

## DID YOU KNOW?

Powerful magnets are kept in very cold temperatures to keep their domains still and their magnetic forces lined up.

To prevent magnets from losing their magnetism too quickly, bar magnets are placed side by side with opposite poles near. Soft iron "keepers" are put across the ends of the bar magnets to provide a loop of opposite poles for the magnetism to follow, and this helps to preserve it.

# Static electricity

Some objects can seem to be attracted in the same way as magnets and magnetic material, but what is pulling them together is not magnetism, it is **static electricity**. Static electricity occurs when certain materials rub together. It happens because everything contains **electrons**, which are so tiny they are invisible. When certain materials rub together, electrons move between them and one material ends up with more than the other. We say it is negatively **charged** and the other is positively charged.

As with the domains in a magnet, unlike or opposite charges attract and like charges repel. So, when you rub a balloon on your hair the balloon attracts your hair, but if you try to put two rubbed balloons together they would try to push away from each other.

Magnetism isn't the only force that can pull things toward each other — in this case static electricity is pulling the girl's hair into the air!

# What Are Magnetic Fields?

A **magnetic field** is the invisible area around a magnet where the magnet's force can attract or repel other magnetic materials. Every magnet is surrounded by a magnetic field. The shape of a magnetic field can be shown with lines drawn from the north pole of a magnet to the south pole. These are called magnetic field lines. Field lines also indicate strength of magnetism. A stronger magnetic field is indicated when the field lines are closer together.

You can see a magne[tic] field by sprinkling iro[n] filings (little pieces of iron) around a magne[t.]

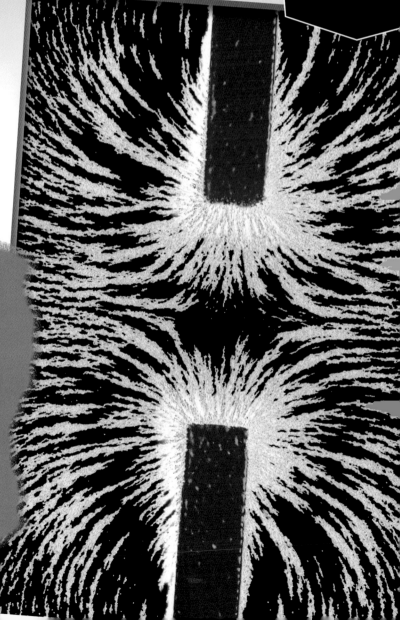

## DID YOU KNOW?

A magnetic field will always have two poles. If you divide a magnet you don't get one piece with a south pole and one piece with a north pole, you get a smaller magnet with two opposite poles. The only thing that changes is its strength.

# Field strength

When you look at field lines around a magnet, the ones that are closest together are at the poles, because that's where the magnetic force on an object is strongest. The strength of magnetic field also depends on how close you are to the magnet. The force is strongest close to the magnet and gets weaker as you move away. That's why you have to hold a small, weak magnet very close to things before it works. As we have seen, other magnetic fields spread wider and are strong enough to work through some materials and even hold up a chair!

## WHAT'S NEXT?

New magnetic refrigerators use strong magnetic fields to increase the temperature of special metals. When the field is removed, the metals cool quickly to a lower-than-starting temperature and can be used to keep food cool!

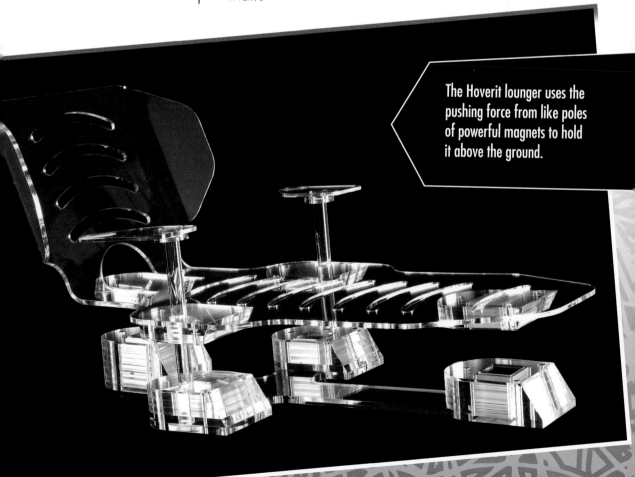

The Hoverit lounger uses the pushing force from like poles of powerful magnets to hold it above the ground.

## Magnetic Earth

The largest magnetic field in the world is around the Earth itself. Our planet behaves like a giant magnet. That's because the center, or **core**, of the Earth is made up of hot, molten (melted) rocks containing magnetic materials such as nickel and iron. The magnetic poles of the Earth are located near the North and South Poles (the Arctic and Antarctic), which is how the poles of magnets got their name.

## Eureka moment!

In 1600, English doctor William Gilbert showed that the world itself was a giant magnet. He set up a magnetic needle so that it could swing freely and found that the north pole of the needle pointed toward the ground.

We can use compasses to find our way because compass needles (and the north poles of all magnets) always point to Earth's magnetic north pole, which is near Earth's geographic North Pole.

## Magnetism in space

The Earth's magnetic field stretches far out into space, into a region called the **magnetosphere**. The magnetosphere helps to create displays of glowing, multicolored lights in the sky. These are known as aurora borealis around the north magnetic pole and aurora australis around the south magnetic pole. These happen when tiny **particles** from the sun flow through the magnetosphere and interact with substances in the atmosphere.

The incredible light shows in the sky known as auroras are usually seen near the Earth's magnetic poles because Earth's magnetic field bends inward and is the strongest at these points.

21

## Animal magnetism

Some animals can probably detect the Earth's magnetic field and use it to find their way around. Scientists think these animals have small amounts of magnetic material in their bodies, which are sensitive to variations in the angle or strength in the magnetic field at different points around the Earth. For example, they may sense a strong pull near the North Pole and a weaker one further south. Sensing these differences helps the animals decide on or correct the route they are taking.

## Eureka moment!

In 1957, German scientist Hans Fromme noticed that robins kept in a dark room at Frankfurt zoo were fluttering to the southwest corner when it was the time of year they would **migrate** if free. He realized they must be acting on the invisible magnetic field of the Earth.

Bees use the Earth's magnetic field to help them find their way around. Then they do a waggle dance to show other bees how to get back to flowers they find to feed on.

## WHAT'S NEXT?

new invention that attaches
magnets to fishing lines could save
thousands of sharks a year from
accidental death. The strong magnets
create magnetic fields that repel
certain types of sharks and stops
them from getting caught on hooks.

This picture shows the route
the turtles take on their
migration and how they use
the angle of the field lines to
help them find their way.

## Migration patterns

Many animals, including bats,
whales, bees, and salmon, are
believed to use Earth's magnetic
field to help them **navigate**! Some
travel enormous distances. After
baby loggerhead turtles hatch
out of their eggs on the shores
of eastern Florida, they set out
on a huge migration that takes
five to ten years. These tiny sea
turtles travel 8,000 miles (12,900
kilometers) clockwise around the
Atlantic Ocean all alone. Scientists
think they inherit a sort of magnetic
map from their parents that helps
them sense which way to go.

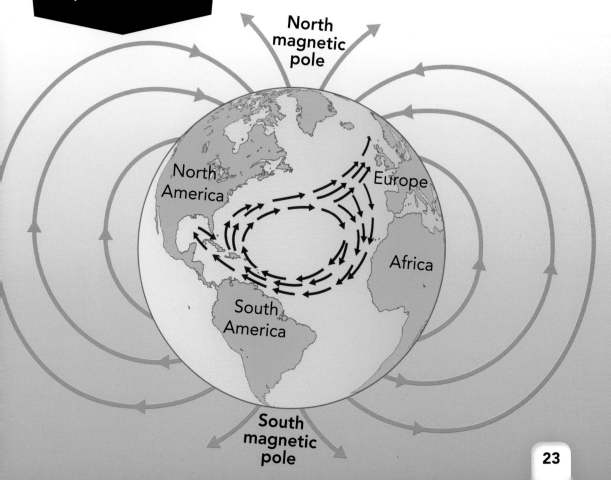

# Try This!

A magnetic field can change the path of a moving metal object by attracting it from a distance.

## Prediction

The magnetic field around a magnet will attract small, light ball bearings more than heavier ones.

## Equipment

- narrow cardboard tube around 20–24 inches (50–60 cm) long (for example from wide aluminum foil or wrapping paper)
- clean food can
- sand
- sticky tape
- steel ball bearings of three different sizes and weights: large, medium, and small (they all need to be able to roll through the tube)
- large, shallow plastic tray
- large piece of paper that fits on the tray
- powerful horseshoe magnet
- ruler and pencil
- poster paint in a shallow dish

## What you do

**1** Pour enough sand into the can to weigh it down so it stands without easily toppling. Rest one end of the tube on the can with the other end on the ground.

**2** Tape the tube to the top of the food can. This is your ball bearing launcher.

24

**3** Lay the paper on the tray on a level table. Position the launcher so the lower end is just on one of the short sides of the paper.

**4** Roll each ball bearing in turn down the tube. Each should travel in a straight line the length of the paper. Use the ruler and pencil to draw the straight path that the bearings take.

**5** Now rest the magnet on the paper. It should be positioned 5 inches (10 cm) from the lower end of the tube and 2 inches (5 cm) to one side of the line you drew. The ends of the magnet should be facing the straight line.

**6** Roll each bearing in turn down the tube. You should find that the magnetic field from the magnet attracts the bearings and makes them travel in a curved path from the launcher. Try to draw the path for each bearing on the paper.

## Results

The magnetic field around the magnet attracts the smallest, lightest ball bearing more than the heaviest one. Its path will also be more curved than that of the medium and large bearings.

Do the different bearings take different paths? You can try to draw the paths using the pencil. Or, if you don't mind the mess, by dipping each bearing in the paint and then letting it roll!

# How Do Electromagnets Work?

An **electromagnet** is a type of magnet in which the magnetic field is created by the flow of electricity. When electricity flows through a wire, it creates a magnetic field around it. If you wind the wire into a tight coil around an iron bar, the electric current **magnetizes** the iron. This combines with the magnetic field of all the turns of the coiled wire and makes the magnetic field stronger. This forms an electromagnet.

## DID YOU KNOW?

Most permanent magnets a... made by putting a steel cor... inside coiled wire instead of iron. When an electric current passes though the coiled wire, it magnetizes the steel, but unlike iron, th... steel keeps its magnetism once the electric current is turned off.

When electric current stops flowing through wire, the nail will no longer be magnetic and will drop the paper clips!

# What's the difference?

Electromagnets have two main advantages over permanent magnets. Permanent magnets stay magnetic all the time, but electromagnets can be switched on and off because they stop working when the electric **current** is turned off. We can also change the strength of an electromagnet by increasing or decreasing the electric current and changing the number of coils in the wire. This means it can make a stronger magnetic field than a permanent magnet of similar size and weight.

## WHAT'S NEXT?

Scientists believe that planets like Earth were formed by tiny particles smashing into each other at high speeds and joining together. To test this complex theory, some scientists have been smashing particles together inside a 16-mile (27-kilometer) circular tube called the Large Hadron Collider in an underground laboratory. To do this they are using the force of 9,300 magnets!

The Large Hadron Collider is kept underground, under the French-Swiss border near Geneva, and it contains giant magnets like this!

# Electric motors

An electric motor is a machine that converts electricity into motion. Most electric motors work by electromagnetism. Inside an electric motor, an electromagnet is placed inside a permanent magnet. When electricity flows through the electromagnet, its magnetic field pushes and pulls against the magnetic field of the permanent magnet. This makes the electromagnet spin around.

## DID YOU KNOW?

The electricity that flow into motors passes through a part called a commutator. This chang the direction in which the electricity moves every half turn, to keep the coil turning in the same direction.

In this simple motor, the wire carrying the electricity is a loop. The two sides of the loop are at right angles to the magnetic field of the permanent magnet, which pulls and repels to make the electromagnet turn. Real motors have coils of wire with many turns to increase the magnetic field.

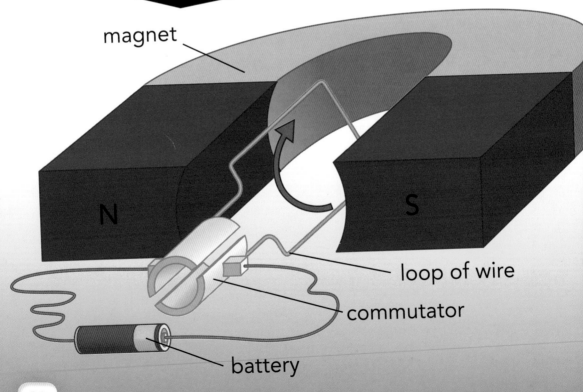

magnet

N

S

loop of wire

commutator

battery

# Motors in action

When electricity makes an electromagnet spin, it can be connected to other parts of a machine to make them move too. Then the motor can be used to drive machines such as hairdryers, food mixers, drills, and vacuum cleaners. In an electric drill, an electric motor makes the bit at the end of the drill spin at high speed to drill holes in walls, wood, and even metal. The motor of a vacuum turns the blades of a fan. The rotating fan sucks in air, and dust, and dirt from carpets. The dirty air goes into a bag that has very tiny holes in it, which traps the dirt and dust and lets clean air escape.

## Eureka!

In 1978, English inventor James Dyson realized his vacuum cleaner was losing suction because of dust clogging up the bag. He invented the Dyson vacuum cleaner that spins dirty air in a cylinder to separate off the dirt, rather than a bag.

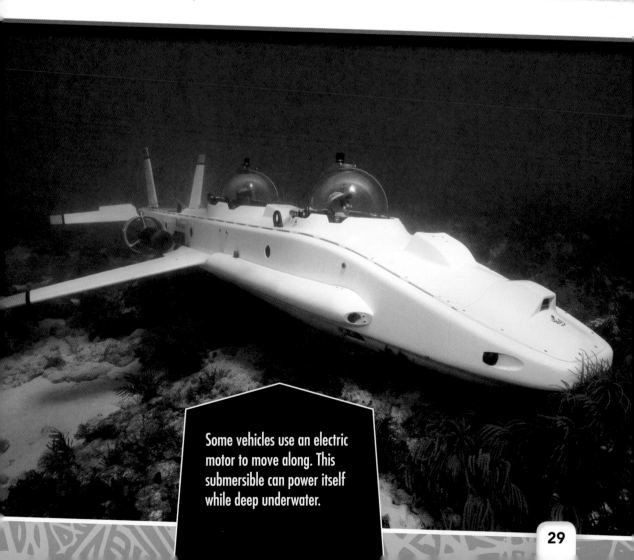

Some vehicles use an electric motor to move along. This submersible can power itself while deep underwater.

# Magnets making electricity

Electricity can make magnetism, and magnetism can make **electricity** too. Electricity is the flow of tiny, electrically charged particles called **electrons**. Everything in the world is made up of **atoms**. Electrons are even smaller parts that are part of atoms. A changing magnetic field can cause electrons to move. By moving a magnet in a coil of wire, the changing magnetic field makes electrons flow in the wire. This is an electric **current**.

## Eureka!

In 1831, both British scientis[t] Michael Faraday and American scientist Joseph Henry discovered that when you change a magnetic field, you can create an electric current. Faraday got the fame for this discovery because he was the first of them to publish a scientific paper with his observations!

When you turn the handle on a wind-up flashlight, this turns a magnet quickly through coiled wires. This creates an electric current in the wires that makes th[e] flashlight work.

## More power

To increase the amount of electric current, you can increase the number of turns or coils in the wire or use a stronger magnet. It is useful to be able to control the strength of an electromagnetic field. For example, an induction cooker is a type of cooker that works using electromagnetism. We control the electromagnetic field to control how hot the pan gets—instantly.

## WHAT'S NEXT?

In the future, our cars could be fitted with magnets so that as they move over roads that contain coils of wire, they can help produce electricity!

Under the surface of an induction cooker, there's a coil of copper wire. When electric current passes through this wire, it creates an electromagnetic field of energy. This passes into pans containing magnetic material such as iron. This makes the pans heat up and cook food.

# Generators

**Power stations** are factories where huge amounts of electricity are made. Power stations use vast magnets inside machines called **generators** to make, or generate, this electricity. In a generator, a big coil of copper wire spins inside huge magnets. As the wire spins, magnetic fields push and pull electrons within it to create electric current. This current flows into power lines that carry it to homes and other buildings all over the country. Power stations use giant wheels, called **turbines**, to spin the coils of wire in generators.

These are the giant blades of a turbine in a power station, used to spin coils of wire inside a generator to make electricity.

## WHAT'S NEXT?

In the future we might be charging phones and MP3 players with miniturbines inside household water pipes. These turbines will turn when water passes through them to generate small amounts of electricity.

# Turning turbines

It takes a lot of energy to spin turbines. Power stations use different systems or **fuels** to get that energy. Many power stations burn coal or use **nuclear power** to boil water and produce steam, like the steam you see blasting out of a kettle. When this steam hits the blades of a turbine, it makes the turbine spin and the turbine rotates the coils of wire. Hydropower stations use fast-moving water to turn turbines and power generators. The huge blades of the turbines on top of wind farm towers use the energy in moving air to turn their blades.

## Eureka!

In 1888, American inventor Charles Brush built the first wind turbine, which was able to generate enough electricity to power all the lights and motors in his large mansion in Ohio.

ind turbine blades are ge so that they can tch as much of the nd's energy as possible. fact, some are longer an a football field!

# What Do We Use Electromagnets For?

We can use electromagnets to make and hear music. Sound is made by vibrations in the air. When we pluck the steel string of an electric guitar, it vibrates. The guitar's pickup has a bar magnet with fine wire coiled around it thousands of times. The string's vibrations cause vibrations in the magnet's magnetic field and a vibrating electric current in the coiled wire, which goes to a speaker.

Inside a speaker, there's another electromagnet and a fixed permanent magnet. As the pulses of electricity go through the coil of the electromagnet, the direction of its magnetic field quickly changes so it is attracted to and repelled from the permanent magnet. The magnet attracts and repels a speaker cone, making it vibrate. The cone then vibrates the air, making the signals come out of the speaker louder, so you can hear them.

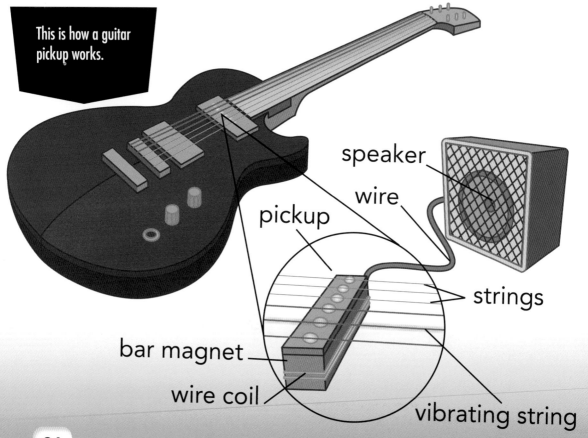

This is how a guitar pickup works.

speaker

wire

pickup

bar magnet

wire coil

strings

vibrating string

# Storing information

Electromagnets are used to store information too, on things such as computer hard drives and credit cards. Credit cards have a magnetic strip on the back containing information about the card and cardholder. When the information is needed again, it can be read back by a magnetic reader. A computer hard disk drive has a coating of iron oxide. By repeatedly turning an electromagnet on and off, the magnetic field magnetizes tiny sections of the iron oxide to store information such as music, film, or words. When you want to see it, another electromagnet converts the magnetic information into electrical signals that show up on your computer screen.

## DID YOU KNOW?

Many electromagnetic devices are sensitive to magnetic fields. People can ruin their credit cards or erase their hard drive by bringing a magnet too close!

This arm is reading the information stored by an electromagnet in a computer hard drive.

# Magnets and medicine

Doctors can use electromagnets to see inside people! An MRI (magnetic resonance imaging) scanner is made up of a large, powerful, tube-shaped magnet. Most of the human body is made up of water, which consists of tiny hydrogen and oxygen atoms. Each hydrogen atom contains an even smaller part called a **proton**. Protons are very sensitive to magnetic fields. When a patient lies in the MRI scanner, the powerful electromagnets create **radio waves** that cause the protons to move. As this happens, each proton sends out a radio wave that provides information about where it is in the body.

## DID YOU KNOW?

MRI scanners contain very strong magnets. Patients have to remove any jewelry or other metal objects before a scan to stop the metal items from suddenly being pulled toward the machine o hitting the patient.

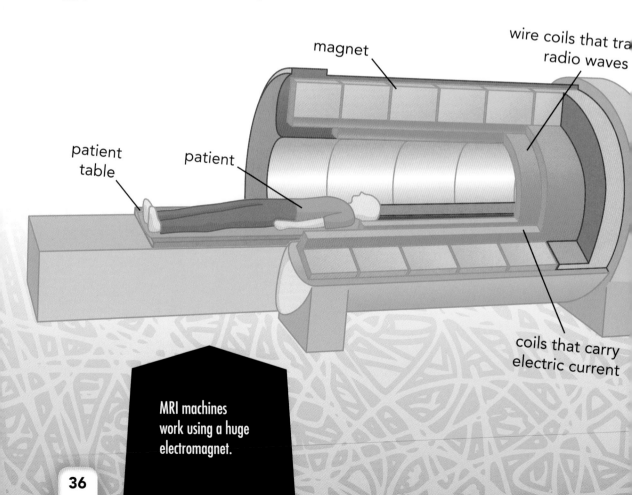

magnet

wire coils that tra radio waves

patient table

patient

coils that carry electric current

MRI machines work using a huge electromagnet.

## Making images

The MRI scanning machine collects together all the radio signals from millions of protons around the body and combines them to make a detailed image of the inside of the body. X-ray machines make good images of hard body parts such as bones, but not other body parts. The advantage of MRI machines is that they make images of the softer body parts, such as blood and the brain.

## Eureka!

In 2009, American scientists invented a way to give people medicine without them visiting hospitals for injections. A special, tiny pouch of medicine is put into their body. When a magnetic field is switched on outside the body, this warms the pouch and opens tiny holes in it, releasing some medicine into the body.

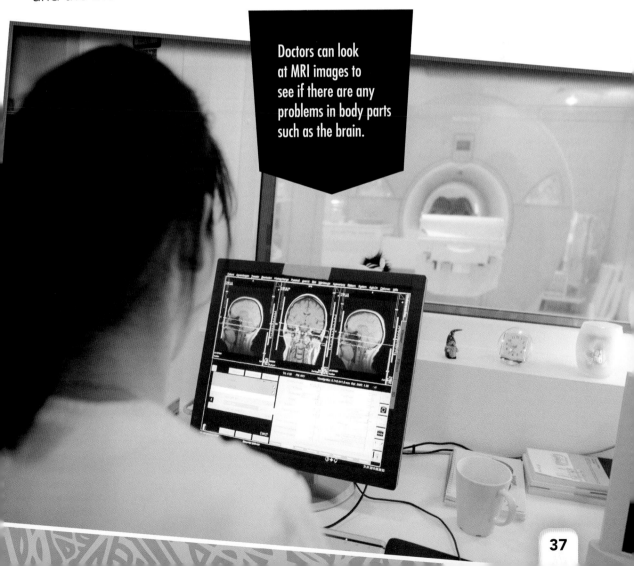

Doctors can look at MRI images to see if there are any problems in body parts such as the brain.

# Magnets and transportation

Maglev trains are trains that operate without touching the tracks! Maglev is short for magnetic levitation, and these trains use electromagnetism to levitate, or float, above a track. Maglev trains use the repelling and attracting forces created by coils of magnetized wire in the tracks and magnets on the underside of the train to lift the train above the track. Electromagnets are also used to move the train forward. When the magnets ahead of the train are polar opposites of those on the train, magnetic forces pull the train forward. Magnets with the same **polarity** as those on the train can push it from behind!

## DID YOU KNOW?

Because the Maglev train is floating just above the track there is no **friction** between tracks and wheels to slow the train down. On test runs, some Maglevs have reached speeds of up to 361 miles (581 km) per hour!

Maglev trains use less energy and create less noise and **pollution** than traditional trains, but the tracks are very expensive to build.

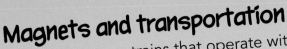

# Magnets on the move

Many rollercoasters launch cars off quickly, rather than climbing gradually, using the repelling forces of strong magnets. Many rollercoasters also use magnets for braking, where magnets attract each other gradually to slow down the cars smoothly. Designers are also working on cars that could be propelled forward by electromagnetism, in a similar way to Maglev trains. The only trouble is that they will need magnetic roads to run on!

## WHAT'S NEXT?

Indian designer K. R. Nanish has come up with an electromagnetic car for the future. Each of its wheels is made of two rings, one an electromagnet and the other a permanent magnet. As the electromagnet is activated by power from the battery, it has the same polarity as the permanent magnet, and this creates a repulsive force to move the wheels.

Rollercoasters can use magnets to launch cars forward at speeds of up to 60 mph (100 kph) in a matter of seconds!

Maglev trains are big, complicated machines with incredibly powerful magnets, but you can make "wheels" levitate too.

## Prediction

I can demonstrate the basic principles behind Maglev trains with a pencil, rulers, and ring magnets.

## Equipment

- 6 donut or ring magnets
- pencil sharpened at both ends (be careful not to poke yourself)
- modeling clay
- 2 short plastic rulers

## Method

**1** Choose a suitable hard surface to carry out the demonstration—remember that modeling clay can leave greasy marks!

**2** Find out which is the north and which is the south pole side of each magnet.

**3** Stand up two of the ring magnets on their edges on lumps of clay to stick them to the surface. The same pole should be upward for each magnet and they should have a gap of about 0.5 inch (1 cm) between them.

Repeat with two more magnets 4 inches (10 cm) away from the first pair.

**4** Using large lumps of clay, stand up the two rulers around 1 inch (2.5 cm) from the pairs of magnets. These are to rest the pencil points against as the pencil spins.

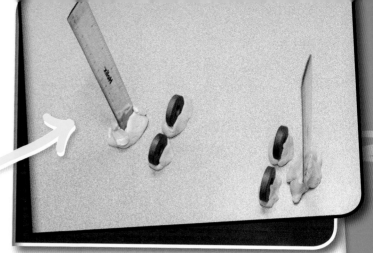

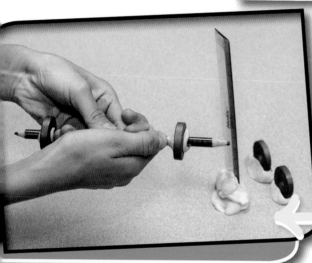

**5** Slide two ring magnets onto the pencil and fix them 4 inches (10 cm) apart using small lumps of clay.

**6** Now position the pencil over the magnets. The ones on the table should repel those on the pencil so that the pencil floats. Adjust the rulers so they just grip the pencil ends. Now spin your wheels!

## Results

The "floating" occurs because the same poles face and thus repel each other. If you spin your pencil it will spin for a long time because there is very little friction to stop it.

# What Has Magnetism Done for Us?

Magnetism has transformed the world. Navigational devices, from simple compasses to GPS systems, all need a piece of metal that is highly sensitive to the Earth's magnetic field to work. Without magnets there would be no speakers, telephones, televisions, or computers.

Without magnets there would be no electric motor and that would mean no washing machines, vacuum cleaners, food mixers, or hairdryers. Without magnetism there would be no electricity! The only source of electricity that doesn't currently require magnets is solar, but solar only generates a tiny proportion of the world's power at present. So, without magnetism we wouldn't have any electric lights or other electric machines either.

Magnetism is used in machines that we use every day and some that we may use more in the future, like this electric car powered by an electric motor that relies on magnets to work.

# Magnets in the future

There are issues with using **fossil fuels** such as coal to generate electricity. There is a limited amount of these fuels, and burning them causes **pollution** and **global warming**. In the future, magnetism may be able to help solve this problem too! Fusion power uses magnetic fields to keep in place materials that are heated to extreme temperatures to power generators and make electricity. And in the future, more transportation systems might rely on magnetism too, perhaps even sending us into space!

## WHAT'S NEXT?

In the future, maglev technology that is currently used to propel trains forward could be used to launch spacecraft into space from magnetic tracks and ramps! The advantage of this system is that it can be used again, unlike rockets that burn up vast amounts of fuel and cannot be reused.

One day magnetic launch systems could be used to send spacecraft into space.

# Glossary

**atom** everything is made up of particles called atoms. Atoms are so small that we cannot see them.

**charge** when something is electrically charged it has electricity in it

**core** the central part of the Earth

**current** when electricity (or a flow of electrons) moves from one place to another, it's called electric current

**domain** area of magnetic force within a material

**electricity** form of energy that we use to power most of the machines we use every day

**electromagnet** magnet that only works when electric current passes through it

**electron** very small part of an atom, with a negative electric charge

**force** effect that causes things to move in a particular way, usually a push or a pull

**fossil fuel** fuel such as coal or oil that was made from plants or animals that died millions of years ago

**friction** action of one object or surface moving across another. Friction is a force that can slow things down.

**fuel** material that produces heat or power, usually when it is burned

**generator** machine that makes electricity

**global warming** increase in the temperature of Earth's atmosphere, probably caused by the burning of fossil fuels such as coal and oil

**magnet** object or material that creates pushing or pulling forces that can attract or repel (push away) some other objects or materials and other magnets

**magnetic field** invisible area around a magnet or electromagnet in which the force of magnetism acts

**magnetize** to make something magnetic

**magnetosphere** region of space into which the Earth's magnetic field stretches

**migrate** to move from one part of the world to another

**mineral** substance found in the Earth, but not formed from animal or vegetable matter, such as gold or salt

**motor** device that produces movement to make a machine work and move

**navigate** to find one's way

**nuclear power** powerful form of energy produced by splitting the atoms in a fuel

**particle** extremely tiny piece of material

**permanent magnet** magnet that keeps its magnetic power for a long time

**polarity** the state of having two opposite poles

**pole** one of two points, such as the ends of a magnet, that have opposing magnetic qualities

**pollution** something that adds dirty, harmful, or dangerous substances to air, water, or soil

**power station** factory where electricity is made

**proton** very small part of an atom with a positive charge

**radio wave** type of electromagnetic wave that carries signals. Some radio waves are natural; others are made by machines, like radios

**repel** push away

**static electricity** type of electrical energy that is made when something has too many electrons or protons

**temporary magnet** magnet that is only magnetic as long as it is in the magnetic field of a permanent magnet or an electric current

**turbine** machine with blades that are turned, for example by pressure from steam, water, or wind, in order to make electricity

**vibrate** to move up and down, or forward and backward

# Find Out More

## Books

Gianopoulos, Andrea. *The Attractive Story of Magnetism with Max Axiom, Super Scientist.* (Graphic Science). Mankato, Minn.: Capstone, 2011.

Kessler, Colleen. *A Project Guide to Electricity and Magnetism* (Physical Science Projects for Kids). Hockessin, Del.: Mitchell Lane, 2011.

Swanson, Jennifer. *The Attractive Truth about Magnetism* (Fact Finders: LOL Physical Science). Mankato, Minn.: Capstone, 2012.

Taylor-Butler, Christine. *Experiments with Magnets and Metals* (My Science Investigations). Chicago: Heinemann-Raintree, 2012.

Walker, Sally M. *Investigating Magnetism* (Searchlight Books: How Does Energy Work?). Minneapolis: Lerner Classroom, 2011.

Weakland, Mark. *Magnets Push, Magnets Pull* (Science Starts). Mankato, Minn.: Capstone, 2011.

## Web sites

**www.bbc.co.uk/learningzone/clips/magnets-and-their-invisible-force/2185.html**
This British BBC learning zone site has science clips about magnetism.

**www.brainpop.com/science/motionsforcesandtime/magnetism/preview.weml**
Here you can watch videos to learn more about the basics of magnets and magnetism.

**www.exploratorium.edu/snacks/iconmagnetism.html**
This web site has lots of ideas for experiments and activities using magnets and magnetism.

**www.fossweb.com/modules3-6/MagnetismandElectricity/**
Visit this site and build your own virtual electromagnet!

# Places to visit

You can investigate the connection between electricity and magnetism by experimenting with how magnets work at the Museum of Science and Industry in Chicago.

The Exploratorium, in San Francisco, examines many different aspects of science and offers hands-on activities.

The American Museum of Science and Energy, in Oak Ridge, Tennessee, offers fun exhibits and hands-on activities that explore energy in many different forms.

The SPARK Museum of Electrical Invention, in Bellingham, Washington, features interactive exhibits that examine the history and science of electricity.

The Museum of Life and Science in Durham, North Carolina, has hands-on activities that take visitors through the process of using scientific tools and conducting scientific inquiry.

At the Science Museum of Minnesota, in St. Paul, you can carry out science experiments! The Bakken Museum, in Minneapolis, is a museum and library devoted to electricity and magnetism.

The Franklin Institute, in Philadelphia, has a lot of basic electromagnetic experiments that you can play with.

# Further research

Why not research more about the history of compasses and how they transformed global shipping transportation? You could also find out why ship's compasses looked different in order to solve the problem of accuracy in rough seas and high waves. Find out why your compass might not work properly if you're standing near an electrical system or in a ship made of iron!

# Index